The Cats Who Adopted Me

"A pet is a loving friend from God."

Carmen Anderson-Harris

Print information available on the last page

Rev. date: 01/29/2019

To order additional copies of this book, contact:
Xlibris
1-888-795-4274
www.Xlibris.com
Orders@Xlibris.com

This Book is given to:

Name:

From:

For more information, write:

57 Gamewell Lane

Willingboro, NJ 08046

609-871-4011

To all pet lovers:
Love with children begins
With a pet. Do you have one?
Enjoy them...

Biography for Carmen Anderson-Harris

Carmen worked for the Willingboro Board
of Education in various departments,

but her joy was to work with children and
encourage them to do their best.

Carmen works as a trained healthcare worker
with Virtua Health and Bayada nurses.

Helping folks to aspire and reach higher
heights is what excites her.

Carmen works with her church and
continues to inspire the youth.

She takes short term missions trips to help
others in various countries around the world.

You can find her six books where books are sold.

The funds from the books support Missions
and communities around the world.

I don't know why I called her Sally,
but the name stuck, and she lifts her
head when I call her name.
Sally was a black and white *bringled* cat.
She had soft hair and meowed softly,
like she was trying to say,
"Will you take me in?"

Sally adapted to me and the landscape wonderfully.
She loved meal time, because at those times
I gave her a little head rub, stroking from her head to her tail.
She was funny too; just like Mr. Whiskers, but in a different way.

As my hands came down her back to her tail,
Sally would arch her back and stiffen her tail
delightfully as if she was saying,
"More, more, I like that, please don't stop!"

Time went by with my new friend until I noticed she was fat.
My neighbor, Miss Ann, told me Sally
was going to have babies. Wow!
I asked, "How and when did this happen?"
Well, only God knows these things for certain.
Could you tell?

Sally got bigger and bigger; her belly
was almost to the ground.
She began to eat less on some days,
or wouldn't come out of her hiding
place for one to three days.
By the way, Sally, like Mr. Whiskers, did
not belong to anyone I knew.
They just stopped by and remained outside,
doing what outside cats do.
Do you know what they do?

Outside cats are not real pets or domesticated.
That means they do not live inside anyone's
home. They come and go on their own time.
They know they're loved, they get fed and
rubbed, so they're content with that.
That makes me sad, for I always wonder
where they go when they're not with me.
Do they have food? Do they get love from other places?
I hope they do. Do you?

Finally, after many absent days, Sally came to eat.
She drank a lot of water, but didn't eat much,
then she would go back to her kittens.
This went on for many days.

I called Ms. Ann to see the cute kittens, and guess what?
They were five of them; all cute and different colors.
They kept trying to climb on the block in the
yard, jumping on each other playfully,
and kept falling off, and that kept me laughing.
You should have seen them,
All trying to be strong and showing off to their mother.

Sadly, I found out that after a certain age Sally
got them to go make their own lives.
It was funny to see their mother snap
at them while they were eating.
I had to learn about this behavior of cats.
Yes, everyone, even humans, must leave
home to make their own life.
Sally was making sure her babies also knew this,
That it was time for them to make life on their own.
Leaving home must be sad, but it's the
way of life and how God planned it.

Sally had two kittens leave. One I named Ginger,
because he was a lovely ginger color.
The other I named Decker, who was a girl.
Ginger finally got adopted and I hope he has a good home.
I hope he is well-behaved and will remember me.
Decker grew into a beautiful girl cat.
One day, her mother went away, and I never saw her again.
Sally and all her babies parted, and I hope and pray that
They are all doing well with their new family.

Decker has stayed with me the longest
of all the cats who came to visit.
Decker is loving, sensitive, enjoys a rub down,
and likes her head to be scratched.
She leans her head to the side when she
wants to be rubbed more. Funny, right?
I love to oblige her too, for she makes me smile.

I talk with Decker more than the other cats
because she shows me more affection.
She enjoys the talks and the rubs.
Sometimes, Decker runs and jumps like
she is catching something in the air.
She looks at me and rolls on her back in the grass,
She knows I like it when she puts on a show.

Decker enjoys dry meat mix, and you
can hear her crunching the food.
Her teeth are sharp and pointed.
After eating, she licks water from her bowl and stretches.
All her behavior is funny, and I am
appreciating learning about cats.

When Decker sleeps on the mat by the back door,
She is on her side or partially on her back.
She looks funny, but then I think she can
wake up quickly if she hears something,
Or if she thinks something is coming to frighten her.
Last week, another cat came to steal her
food and I heard a noise outside.
I went to investigate, and decker was
chasing the grey cat away.
It was a good thing that she was protecting her things.

New additions came in 2018, when I found out
Decker was expecting her new family.
One day I saw a black and white cat with
a collar looking very distinguished.
It seemed like he was courting Decker all the time.
Decker was expecting; when, I didn't know.
I tried to make a bed for her and hoped
she would be a good mother.
Do you think she would?

Decker did some of the same things
as her sisters before her.
She did not eat all the time and she
needed more loving from me.
She would look in my face as if she
knew what I was saying to her.
Some of the things I said were,
"Is the black cat the father of the babies?"
or "Why do you need a family?"
Sometimes I found that Decker was allowing her boy
cat friend to eat her food while she looked on.
She did not chase him away like she used to.
Love makes you accept things as they are,
especially when you can't change the situation.

Decker kept visiting with the black and white cat,
the father of the babies. Let's call him Sammy.
He never stays when he sees me.
He sometimes hides nearby and hopes I will go
back inside, or he just goes back home.
How fascinating their love story is.

At last, Decker had her four kittens, and
she didn't show them to anyone.
For at least a month, Decker was very
protective of her babies.
She comes to eat, but she is always watching
in the direction of her babies.
When she thinks they are in danger, she
scurries quickly to protect them.
All mothers are like that, they protect when there's danger.

Weeks have passed and still no sign of the kittens.
One day, I tiptoed to see if I could find
the hideaway where they were.
Guess what? I heard noises and cries,
so I got a glimpse of the babies.
There were four of them, and they were beautiful.
There were two grey ones, one black and white, and
the other striped; but all of them were lovely.
After my joyous time seeing them, I
walked away and told Ms. Ann.
She was excited about them, too.

Decker is a good mother.
She loves to come to eat and trots
right back to her babies.
She makes sure she is eating and
drinking so she can nurse them.
This way they can become stronger
and come eat for themselves.
What a day that will be when Decker and
four babies will come meet me.
I can't wait!

Yesterday, after a very long wait, Decker and
the babies came out of their house.
They began to play openly, and I was thrilled
to see them chasing each other.
They climbed on each other with playful joy.
Oh, I wish you could see them, they would make you smile,
Or make you want to get in on the
games they were playing, too.
Life can be fun, you must enjoy every
moment you have on earth.
God would want you to; that's why He gave you life.

Decker's kittens don't have names yet.
They have not come close enough for me to touch them.
Whenever I get close, they all run to hide
where they are protected and feel safe.
When Decker's kitten come out to play, she
lays in the garden bed, watching.
They know she is close by.
I know this because Decker makes a soft meow.
Very gentle, as if letting them know she is
watching and enjoying their playing.
Decker's flashes her tail gently, also
showing her good motherly joys.

Decker also growls when I think the kittens are naughty.
She lets them know she is not pleased
in what they are doing.
Another thing she does is meow in a different
way when they are not playing,
And she wants to know what they are up to.
As soon as she makes this different sound
in her meowing, guess what?
They come to her and then she smells each one,
Licking, cleaning, and grooming them.
Decker really takes good care of her kittens.
I love her for her tenderness, care, and love.

Playing Kittens

Love is kind and tender; a good thing for all.

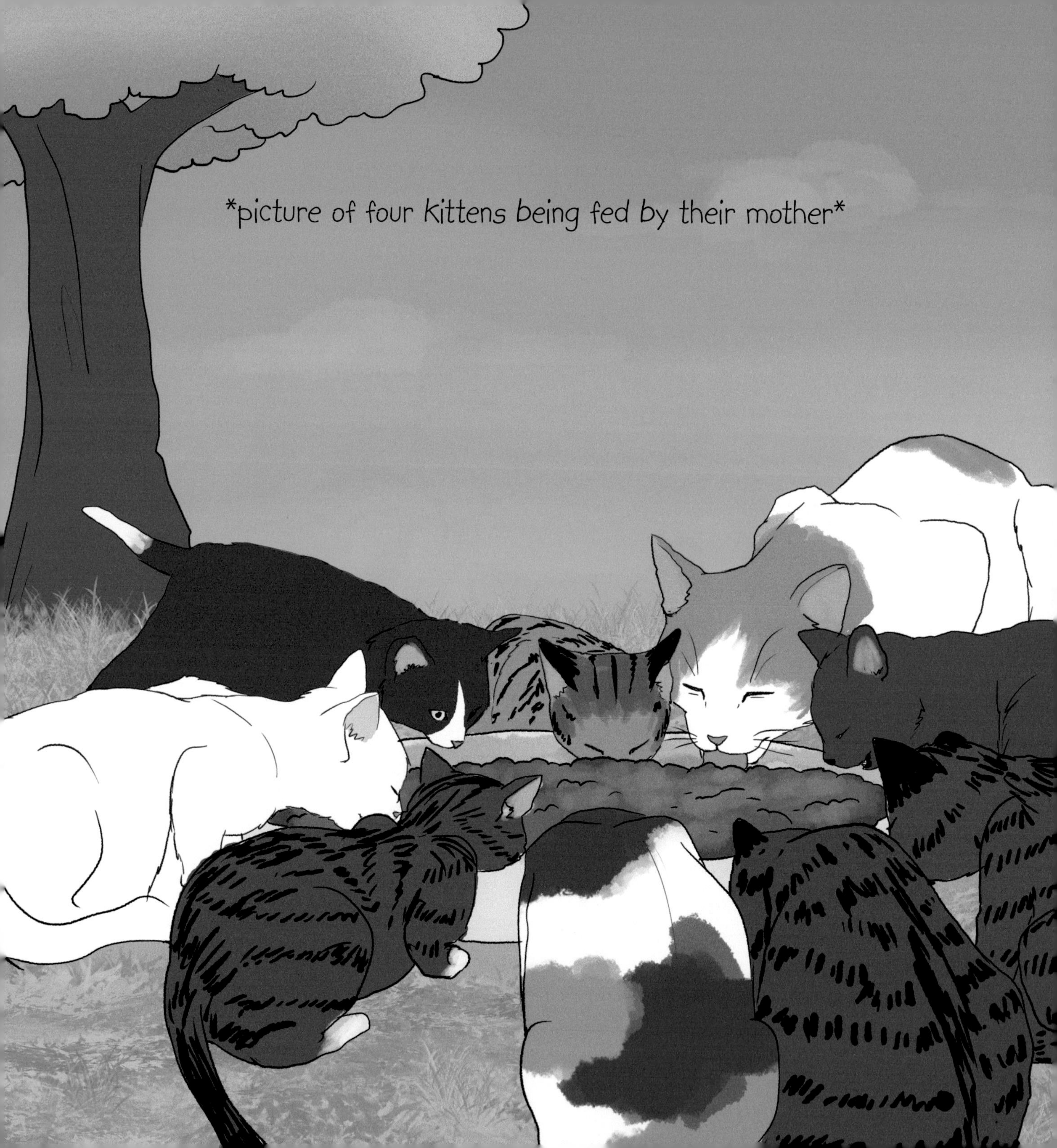
picture of four kittens being fed by their mother

Decker continues to feed her babies,
Because they're unable to eat her food, the meat mix.
Their teeth are not strong enough yet,
But soon, they will enjoy eating out of a
large dish with their mother.

Decker's mother was Sally.

She had a brother named Ginger, and they all
went their separate ways, leaving Decker.

Decker stayed with me, but never became a house cat.

She enjoys the outside where she does whatever she wants.

However, she is loving, smart, and loves to be with me.

Decker has become the community cat
everyone loves and talks about.

Decker enjoys free food at Ms. Ann's house, too.

At times I see her bore through the fence to her yard.

How smart it is to get food from both homes.

Decker's life with me is a good life, we
enjoy each moment we have.
I do not know when she will leave my property, but until then,
she is always a joy to have as I watch her play,
chase the birds, and sneak up on a mouse.
What a life she lives!
Decker practices sharpening her claws on a butterfly
tree and stretches and grooms herself daily.
She keeps herself clean and her colors are bright
and lovely. She's a beautiful and charming lady.
One day, her babies will grow up and find life for themselves.
Hopefully, Decker will be around for a very
long time as our community joy!

How old is Decker? She is five years old now,
as has become a good and caring mother.
May your love for animals continue to grow.
May you know the joys of caring for at least one
animal and love them as you love people.
Continue to enjoy reading and pass on to read other stories.
Travel the world by reading good books.
Enjoy your knowledge and keep dreaming
of exotic places and inventions.
One day you could be one, too.

You can also call this number

and hear daily stories by Cousin Andy

(Carmen Anderson-Harris)

Cousin Andy's
Bible Story by Telephone

Free Call Sponsored By:
609 871-3448
Applied Bible Concepts Ministries
57 Gamewall Lane
Willingboro, NJ 08046

Printed in the United States
By Bookmasters